PASSPORT BOOKS
NTC/Contemporary Publishing Group

SPANISH FUN

**Hola, soy mexicana.
Me llamo María.**

oh-la soy meh-hee*kah*-na
meh *yah*mo mareea

*Hello, I'm Mexican.
My name is Maria.*

**Hello, I'm American.
My name is Peter.**

Hola, soy americano.
Me llamo Peter.

oh-la soy amairee-*kano*
meh *yah*mo Peter

Catherine Bruzzone
and Lone Morton
Illustrations by Louise Comfort

¡hola!
oh-la
hello, hi

buenos días
boo-ehnoss deeass
good morning

buenas tardes
booeh-nass tar-dess
good evening

buenas noches
booeh-nass noch-ess
good night

adiós
adee-oss
good-bye

hola

hola

buenos días

buenos días

buenas tardes

buenas tardes

buenas noches

buenas noches

adiós

adiós

¡Hola!...

Cut out the Spanish words below. Put them in the speech bubbles and practice the different greetings.
Read them aloud.

Keep the words and you can play the game again.

First write in your name and age. Then fill in the correct ages in Spanish below and read them aloud.

Me llamo Sheila

Tengo setenta **años.**

12

8

Tengo doce **años.**

Tengo Ocho **años.**

2

5

Tengo dos **años.**

7

Tengo cinco **años.**   **Tengo** siete **años.**

Me llamo...
me *yah*mo
My name is...

Tengo ... años.
tengo ... *any*oss
I am ... years old.

1	**uno**	*oo*no
2	**dos**	*doss*
3	**tres**	*trayss*
4	**cuatro**	*kwa*tro
5	**cinco**	*sin*ko
6	**seis**	*sayss*
7	**siete**	see-*eh*teh
8	**ocho**	*ocho*
9	**nueve**	noo*eh*beh
10	**diez**	dee-*ess*
11	**once**	*on*seh
12	**doce**	*dos*eh
13	**trece**	*tres*eh
14	**catorce**	*cator*seh
15	**quince**	*kin*seh
16	**dieciséis**	dee-esee-*sayss*
17	**diecisiete**	dee-esee-see-*eh*teh
18	**dieciocho**	dee-esee-*o*cho
19	**diecinueve**	dee-esee-noo*eh*beh
20	**veinte**	*vayn*teh

You'll find the numbers up to 100 on the inside cover.

¿Dónde está…?

dondeh estah

Where is…?

¿Dónde están…?

dondeh estan

Where are…?

Read these questions aloud in Spanish. Check off the list when you have found each item.

¿Dónde están las montañas? ☐

dondeh estan las montanyass

Where are the mountains?

¿Dónde está el avión? ☐

dondeh estah el abeeyon

Where is the plane?

¿Dónde está el pájaro? ☐

dondeh estah el pah-hah-ro

Where is the bird?

¿Dónde está el barco? ☐

dondeh estah el barco

Where is the ship?

¿Dónde están las vacas? ☐

dondeh estan las vakass

Where are the cows?

¿Dónde están los peces? ☐

dondeh estan los pes-ess

Where are the fish?

4

¿Dónde está…?

Spanish is spoken in at least 25 countries in the world! Here is a map showing a few of these countries in Latin America. Can you fill in the missing names, in English?

Answers and Spanish pronunciation on the inside cover.

Do you know the colors of the Mexican flag? Find out and color in this flag.

¿Dónde está…?

Mark and Susan are lost. Can you help them find their way to the station? (*Answer on the inside cover.*)
Read the questions in the margin aloud in Spanish.
Find each place on the map and check it off the list.

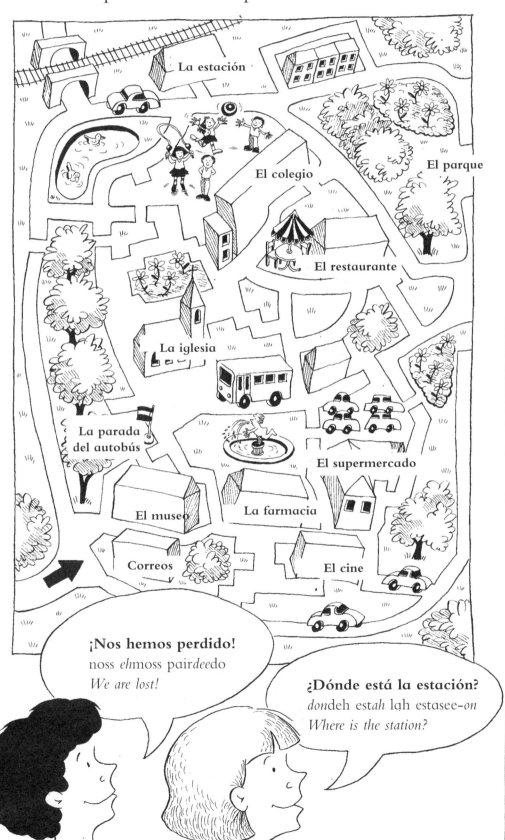

La estación

El colegio

El parque

El restaurante

La iglesia

La parada del autobús

El supermercado

El museo

La farmacia

Correos

El cine

¡Nos hemos perdido!
noss *ehmoss* pair*deedo*
We are lost!

¿Dónde está la estación?
*don*deh est*ah* lah estasee-*on*
Where is the station?

¿Dónde está el parque?
*don*deh est*ah* el *park*eh
Where is the park?

¿Dónde está el colegio?
*don*deh est*ah* el col*eh*-heeo
Where is the school?

¿Dónde está Correos?
*don*deh est*ah* kor*eh*-oss
Where is the post office?

¿Dónde está el cine?
*don*deh est*ah* el *seen*eh
Where is the movie theater?

¿Dónde está el restaurante?
*don*deh est*ah* el rest-ow-*ran*teh
Where is the restaurant?

¿Dónde está el museo?
*don*deh est*ah* el moo*seh*-o
Where is the museum?

¿Dónde está la parada del autobús?
*don*deh est*ah* lah par*ada* del ow-to*boos*
Where is the bus stop?

¿Dónde está el supermercado?
*don*deh est*ah* el supermair-*cah*do
Where is the supermarket?

¿Dónde está la iglesia?
*don*deh est*ah* lah eeg*lay*-seea
Where is the church?

¿Dónde está la farmacia?
*don*deh est*ah* lah far-*mas*eeah
Where is the pharmacy?

…por favor
por fa*vor*   …*please*

5

¿Qué es?

keh ess

What is it?

¿Qué son?

keh sonn

What are they?

Es...

ess

It's...

Son...

sonn

They are...

Es una goma.

ess *oo*nah *go*-ma

It's an eraser.

Son lápices.

sonn *lapee*-sess

They are pencils.

Es una mesa.

ess *oo*nah *meh*-sa

It's a table.

Es una regla.

ess *oo*nah *ray*-gla

It's a ruler.

Es una mochila.

ess *oo*nah mo*cheela*

It's a backpack.

Son libros.

sonn *leebros*

They are books.

Son tijeras.

sonn tee-*hairass*

They are scissors.

Es una silla.

ess *oo*nah *seel*-ya

It's a chair.

¿Qué es?

Join the dots to find out! Count in Spanish as you go.
Then write the answers in Spanish underneath.

The numbers from 21 to 100 and the answers are on the inside cover.

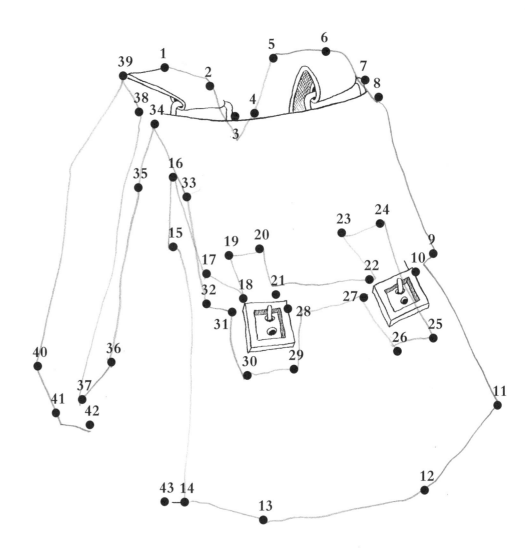

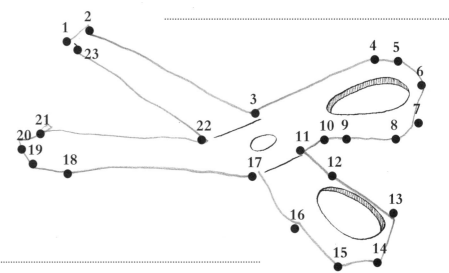

Match these up!

Match up these pictures, then practice saying the words aloud in Spanish. You'll need two dice. Throw one die or two dice, as you like, and say the Spanish name for the picture that corresponds to the number you threw.

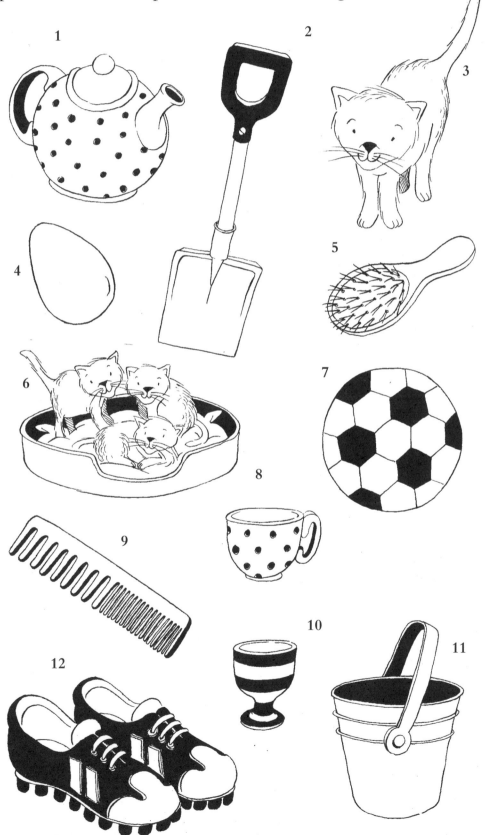

el peine
el *payee*-neh
comb

el gato
el *gat*-o
cat

la huevera
lah ooeh-*vair*ah
egg cup

las botas de fútbol
lass *botass* deh *foot*bol
soccer shoes

los gatitos
loss ga*tee*-toss
kittens

la tetera
lah teh-*taira*
teapot

el cubo
el *coo*-bo
pail

el balón de fútbol
el bal-*lon* deh *foot*bol
soccer ball

el huevo
el *ooeh*-vo
egg

la taza
lah *tas*-a
cup

la pala
lah *pah*-la
shovel

el cepillo para el pelo
el se*peel*-yo *pahra* el *peh*-lo
hairbrush

**Me gusta…/
Me gustan…**

meh *goosta*/me *goostan*
I like…

**No me gusta…/
No me gustan**

no meh *goosta*/
no meh *goostan*
I don't like…

el sol

el sol
sun

los peces

loss *pes*-ess
fish

el castillo de arena

el cas*teel*-yo deh a*reh*-na
sandcastle

las olas

lass *ohlass*
waves

las algas

lass *algass*
seaweed

la sombrilla

lah som*breel*-ya
beach umbrella

el flotador

el flotta-*dor*
float ring

el cangrejo

el kan*greh*-ho
crab

las gaviotas

lass gavee-*otass*
seagulls

la pelota

lah peh-*lota*
ball
8

Me gusta…

Look at this beach scene and circle ten things you like.
Then say them out loud in Spanish.
Start with '**me gusta…**' (singular) or '**me gustan**' (plural).

el suéter
el *sweh*tair
sweater

La ropa
lah *rohpa*
clothes

el sombrero
el som*brair*-o
hat

el vestido
el vest*eedo*
dress

los pantalones
los pantalo-ness
pants

el bañador
el ban*yador*
swimsuit

los calcetines
loss calseh*teen*-ess
socks

los zapatos
loss sap*ah*-toss
shoes

Cut carefully around these clothes to dress the characters. ✂

la camiseta
lah kamee*seh*-ta
T-shirt

la bufanda
lah boo*fan*-da
scarf

el abrigo
el *abreego*
coat

los guantes
los *gwantess*
gloves

los pantalones cortos
loss pantalo-ness *cortos*
shorts

la falda
lah *falda*
skirt

l pijama
pee-*hah*ma
ajamas

las botas
lass *boh*tass
boots

la gorra
lah *go*rrah
cap

No me gusta…

Now circle four things you don't like.
Say them out loud in Spanish. Start with '**no me gusta**'
(singular) or '**no me gustan**' (plural).

¿Cuántos peces?

kwantoss pes-ess

How many fish?

How many fish can you find in the picture?

Answer on the inside back cover.

el sombrero

el sombray-ro

sun hat

la concha

lah koncha

shell

la playa

lah plah-yah

beach

la toalla

lah toh-aya

towel

el barco de vela

el barko deh beh-la

sailboat

el picnic

el peekneek

picnic

el tiburón

el teebooron

shark

el traje de baño

el trah-heh deh banyo

swimsuit

la radio

lah radeeo

radio

las gafas de sol

lass gah-fass deh sol

sunglasses

la medusa

lah medoosa

jellyfish

¿Cuántos?/¿Cuántas?

kwantoss/kwantass

How many?

9

la familia
lah *famee*-leea
family

la madre/mamá
lah *mah*-dreh/mam-*ah*
mother/mom

el padre/papá
el *pah*-dreh/pap-*ah*
father/dad

la hermana
lah air*mah*-na
sister

el hermano
el air*mah*-no
brother

la abuela
lah ab*weh*-la
grandmother

el abuelo
el ab*weh*-lo
grandfather

el bebé
el beh-*beh*
baby

los padres
loss *pah*-dress
parents

la hija
lah *ee*-ha
daughter

el hijo
el *ee*-ho
son

los gemelos
loss he*meh*-loss
twins

10

La familia

Match up the family members. Now label them in Spanish. You may find there is more than one way to describe each person. *Answers on the inside cover.*

1 La hermana el hermano

2 La abuela

3 La hija

4 La madre y le papá

a

b el abuelo

c el hijo

d los gemelos

El café

Practice ordering snacks in a café.
Play this game with a partner. Pretend you are ordering at this café. Use the picture to help you.
The first player orders, say, '**un café, por favor**.'
The next player repeats the order but adds something else, say, '**un café y un helado, por favor**.'
The winner is the last person to say the whole list correctly in the right order.

el café
el *cafeh*
café

un helado
oon el*ah*-do
ice cream

un trozo de pastel
oon *tro*-so deh pas*tell*
a piece of cake

un café con leche
oon *cafeh* con *leh*-cheh
coffee with milk

un té
oon teh
a tea

un bocadillo...
oon boca*deel*-yo
a ... sandwich

...de jamón
deh ham*on*
...ham

...de queso
de *keh*-so
...cheese

un jugo de naranja
oon *hoo*go deh nah*ran*-ha
an orange juice

un chocolate caliente
oon chocolateh calee-*enteh*
a hot chocolate

un vaso de agua
oon *bah*-so deh *ag*wa
a glass of water

¿Cuánto es?
*kwan*to ess?
How much is it?

Quiero...
kee-*airo*
I'd like...

el mercado
el mair*cah*-do
market

tomates
to*mah*-tess
some tomatoes

peras
*pair*ass
some pears

plátanos
plah-tanoss
some bananas

fresas
*frays*ass
some strawberries

zanahorias
sana-*oree*ass
some carrots

manzanas
man*sah*-nass
some apples

patatas
pa*tah*-tass
some potatoes

lechuga
le*choo*ga
some lettuce

un pepino
oon pe*pee*no
a cucumber

cebollas
se*bol*yass
some onions

Quiero...

You are going shopping. Read the two shopping lists aloud. Start with '**quiero....**' Then cut out the items you need below and fill the correct basket.

El mercado

peras
un pepino
tomates
cebollas
zanahorias
patatas
manzanas
fresas

El supermercado

Can you find the coin purse hidden in each picture?

el supermercado
el supermair-*cah*-do
supermarket

jabón
ha*bon*
some soap

champú
cham*poo*
some shampoo

galletas
ga*lay*-tass
some cookies

yogur
yo*goor*
some yogurt

bebidas
beb-*ee*dass
some drinks

azúcar
a*sookar*
some sugar

mermelada
mairmeh-*lah*-da
some jam

mantequilla
manteh-*keelya*
some butter

pan
pan
some bread

patatas fritas a la inglesa
pa*tah*-tass *freetass* ah lah en*gleh*sa
some potato chips

un monedero
oon moneh-*dairo*
a coin purse

mantequilla
mermelada
pan
yogur
champú
azúcar
patatas fritas
galletas

Across

1. Where you would go to buy medicine.
6. The, for more than one thing (two possible answers).
7. One (boy).
8. You drink tea or coffee from it.
9. The (girl).
10. ---, dos, tres.
11. A common greeting.
13. It is very sweet.
15. Shoes for soccer.
16. You see with them.

Down

1. Girls wear it.
2. Where you would go to eat out.
3. Your father's father.
4. You drink this when you are thirsty.
5. ------- fritas a la inglesa.
12. You put sand in it on the beach.
14. The color of tomatoes.
17. It is.

Wordsearch

Find the Spanish for these words, then circle them on the wordsearch. (They are all words you have already seen.)

JAM
MOTHER
WAVES
SHOVEL
BROTHER
BEACH
BUS
BACKPACK
CAT
SUN

14

Crossword & wordsearch

Using the words you have learned in Spanish, fill in this crossword. Then do the wordsearch below.
Answers on the inside cover.

Spot the difference

There are eight differences between these pictures. Can you find them?
How many things can you name in Spanish? The new words are given.

la tienda
lah tee-*enda*

la cometa
lah ko*meh*-tah

las botas
lass *botass*

el flotador
el flotta-*dor*

el pato
el *pah*-to

los patitos
loss pa*teetoss*

el remo
el *reh*-mo

la piragua
lah peer*agwah*

Spanish fortune teller!

First color in the four corners. Then cut out the square along the solid line. Fold back the corners along the diagonal dotted lines. Turn over (so you can read the colors and numbers) and fold back the corners again along the diagonals. Fold in half (backwards) both ways.
Now play!

azul
ah seu oo elóh
blue

5 **cinco**

Ganarás la lotería.
gana-rass lah lotereea
You'll win the lottery.

Eres fuerte.
airess fwaireh
You are strong.

3 **tres**

verde
vehrday oobeh ch aireh deh ch
green

7 **siete**

¡Eres un animal!
airess oon animal
You are an animal!

How to play

1. Insert the finger and thumb of each hand into the four pockets.
2. With the four corners tightly together, ask a friend to choose one of the four colors.
3. Spell out the color in Spanish, opening and closing the *fortune teller* each time. Use the pronunciation guide for the letters of the alphabet. *(The full A-Z is on the inside cover.)*
4. On the final letter, ask your friend to select a number from inside.
5. Then count out the number in Spanish, opening and closing as before.
6. Ask your friend to choose another number, and count it out in Spanish again.
7. Your friend selects a final number and you read the message underneath!

6 **seis**

Tienes suerte.
tee-elmess swaireh
You're lucky.

¡Bésame!
beh-zameh
Kiss me!

4 **cuatro**

Serás muy popular.
sairass mwee poopoolar
You'll be very famous.

2 **dos**

amarillo
ahmah-reeyo ah emeh ah aireh ee eleh eleh o'
yellow

1 **uno**

Tienes gracia.
tee-elmess grah-seea
You're funny.

¡Te quiero!
teh kee-airo
I love you!

8 **ocho**

rojo
roho hota o' aireh o'
red